ICON

The ICONic Chicago Travel Guide

20 Fun Things To Do In Chicago and the Neighboring Suburbs

Anything worth doing, is worth doing
well.

ICON

Contents

1

Chapter 1

O ther than tropical palm trees, the Chicago Metropolis has everything one could ever want or need. So I advise you to protect your heart upon arrival because you may fall in love and have to move! That is what happened to me. I visited a few times and fell in love with the area. At present, I have lived here for over 20 years!

Enough about me! So...you are going on a trip to Chicago... What should you pack? The Chicago area has very temperamental weather. Summer is as intense as winter and it is called 'The Windy City' for a reason. During the winter season it gets really cold but whatever temperature it reaches becomes intensified by the wind. This is called a wind chill factor. It could be -10 degrees and the wind makes it feel like -20 degrees! If you are visiting Chicago in the winter, the first place you need to find when you get in, is a Burlington Coat factory to buy yourself a real winter jacket! This is because unless you are arriving from Moscow, the jacket you have is a joke compared to what you need! The summer weather is as authentic as if you were visiting a tropical Caribbean island! In between these, the summer and winter seasons, you could start off any day with sunny, cool weather and end up with rain! You must pack an umbrella and take it with you every day. Okay, there is a lot of really great Chicago weather too! The key word is temperamental. The weather could start off one way and then change to something else by midday. Be prepared!

In Chicago, no matter the diversity of your palate, your taste buds will have an orgasm over and over again! There is authentic Chinese food, African food, Indian food, Palestinian food, British food, Mexican food e.t.c. The restaurants are as diverse as the people who live in the metropolis! You would be hard pressed to find a more diverse city to visit. If you are into spicy food, you will not have to walk around with a bottle of hot sauce because the cuisine you get will hit the spot with no additional help. If you are into Mediterranean food, never fear, there are a lot of restaurants where they will fire up your food in front of you to your heart's desire. If you love the raw, Japanese dishes, you will be impressed by the many options you have of places to eat. If you are a lover of American steakhouses, you will have a wide variety to choose from.

If you are looking for a city with history, it does not get any better. Whip out the history books! It goes from the Chicago fires many, many years ago, to the inauguration of the 1st black president, President Barack Obama! The city is the home and site for many TV shows and movies! From the present day Chicago series; Chicago Fire, Chicago P.D. and Chicago Med., to The Godfather and our most popular gangster from the past, Al Capone and his neck of the woods, Little Italy!

This book is not going to give you the prices of everything. In the Chicago area, you can go from shopping at extremely affordable grocery stores like Walmart and Target, to eating at expensive restaurants like The Signature Room on the 95th floor! You can rent a horseback carriage ride to take you on a scenic walk down town or jump on the L train to see the downtown sites as they go by! A trip to the Chicago Metropolis can be as cheap or expensive as your budget permits! You can experience the Chicago metropolis to its fullest on any budget!

This is also not a book that must be consumed sequentially, or in its entirety at once. You can pick whichever topic you fancy, and zone in on whatever information you need as your trip unfolds, or you can choose to read the entire book and plan and strategize before you leave for Chicago. It is all up to you!

Welcome to the ICONic Chicago Travel guide! You may not get a chance to enjoy all 20 of the fun things to do in Chicago and the neighboring suburbs in one trip, but you can always come back and visit us again!

20 Fun Things To Do In Chicago And The Neighboring Suburbs (a.k.a. The Chicago Metropolis!)

(1) The Willis Tower :-

Let us kick off our great adventure with the skyscraper formerly known as The Sears Tower! It is located in the center of the downtown area of the city of Chicago. It used to be known as the tallest building in the world! Now it is considered ONE of the tallest buildings in the world. It is exciting to be that elevated and to see the city of Chicago from this vantage point. One can go all the way to the top and view the metropolis from its zenith, the SkyDeck, or if you want something less intense, you can view the city from a floor about midway up. Both views are phenomenal and it is an experience of a lifetime! You can do both!

(2) The Signature Room:-

This is also known as the restaurant where President Barack Obama proposed to Michelle, the first lady! It is located on the 95th floor of the John Hancock building, one of the most popular skyscrapers in the downtown Chicago area. This building is the reason for the phrase " I need your John Hancock over here.." when you are asking a person to put their signature down on something. It is a restaurant with such compelling food and such an amazing view that it brought President Barack Obama to his knees! The rest is history!

Also, the John Hancock building has 360 Chicago, which is a floor that gives you the opportunity to view Chicago from above. It is on the 94th floor. It is the next best thing to viewing Chicago from the Willis Tower!

(3) Take a bike ride on the Lakefront :-

There is a beautiful bike trail on Lakefront of Lake Michigan downtown Chicago. It spans almost the complete length of Lake Shore Drive. It gives such a scenic view for you to experience first hand. From this trail you can see such Chicago landmarks as The Navy Pier and interesting buildings such as the skyscraper where Oprah dwells at times. The experience is just as exciting on foot!

(4) Grant Park & Millennium Park:-

Grant Park is the site of The Chicago Music Festival downtown Chicago. There are many other musical performances that take place at Grant Park throughout the year! The Chicago Music Festival Happens there once a year. Even when there is no ongoing performance, Grant park is a beautiful location to experience and simply hang out. There is iconic outdoor art to be seen! Also, here is where you get the best view of the Chicago skyline as seen on postcards!

Millennium Park is just as popular as Grant Park and has Cloud Gate, a world renowned sculptor by Indian born British artist, Anish Kapoor. Another name for Cloud Gate is " The Bean" as it is more commonly referred to as. Millennium Park is located downtown Chicago. It is a great place to enjoy on foot! These two parks are not far from each other.

(5) Indoor Skydiving :-

For a day of intense adventure, go indoor skydiving! There are 3 locations for this in the Chicago Metropolis! They are the three locations of the Ifly indoor skydiving company. Downtown Chicago, Naperville and Rosemont. All 3 locations are easily accessible. This is a family treat! It is for kids as young as 4 or 5 years old all the way to adults of all ages! Indoor skydiving here simulates outdoor skydiving to a T! It will simply take your breath away! Remember to book it a couple days before you plan on enjoying the experience.

(6) Six Flags Great America Amusement Park :-

Reserve an entire day to enjoy this adventure! At Six Flags there are so many amazing rides to go on and amazing food to try that even if you were to walk in with your family when the gates open and leave right before they close, you would not have the time to try everything! There are so many world famous rides! Some will be thrilling and others might scare you into peeing on yourself! Beware! A handful of the attractions there are Superman, Velocity squared (v2), Batman, The Joker, and The Green Lantern! There are a few calmer rides for the admittedly faint at heart, like the teacups and the water rides.

(7) Spend the day at a Waterpark:-

This is relaxing family friendly fun! There are a lot of water parks in the Chicago metropolis! Most of them have Lazy Rivers and all sorts of splashy, relaxing fun!

Here are a few:-

Rice Pool & Waterpark, Wheaton

Seafari Springs, Hanover Park

Mystic Waters Family Aquatic Center,
  Des Plaines
  Forest Park Aquatic Center, Forest Park
  Sea Lion Aquatic Center, Lisle
  Cypress Cove Family Aquatic Park, Woodridge
  Santa's Village Amusement Park and Water Park, East Dundee

(8) Horseback Riding :-

This makes for a great nature adventure. There are a number of horse riding farms in the Chicago Metropolis. There are those for experienced riders and those for beginners. The locations for beginners have suitably trained staff to make the ride safe, enjoyable and controlled. It is a memorable experience!

(9) Visit historical architecture in Oak Park, Visit the home of President Barack Obama in Hyde Park and stop by Little Italy for some Italian Ice! :-

All in a day trip! Oak Park is known as being home to famous Architect Frank Lloyd Wright. You can go to the suburb of Oak Park and take a tour of his childhood home and visit some other homes he designed. This should take less than two hours and then you can move on to neighboring Hyde Park where you can look at the home of President Barack Obama. After experiencing these two wonderful suburbs you can go to Little Italy in the City of Chicago and sit down to some Italian Ice at any one of the hole in the wall businesses in the neighborhood that sell it! It is great!

Little Italy was the dwelling place of the infamous gangster, Al Capone! A lot of the Italian gangsters of his time lived in a bourgeoisie suburb right beside Oak Park called River Forest.

The high school students in this city converge at a high school in Oak Park called Oak Park River Forest High School (OPRF),a top of the line high school made popular by the movie 'America To Me' which was released in 2018. This movie was made in and about OPRF high school.

(9) Spend a day shopping:-
The Chicago Metropolis is home to so many huge shopping malls.
-Gurnee Mills Mall (one of the largest malls in America)
-Oak Brook Mall
-Old Orchard Mall
Just to name a few that I have frequented. There are also a bunch of popular outlet malls.
Michigan Avenue downtown is home to the incredible Water Tower Mall. As you stroll up and down Michigan avenue on either side of the street there are a lot of world famous clothing stores, perfume and cologne stores, The American Girl doll experience and basically any kind of retail store you fancy! It is awesome! The Buckingham fountain is a great place to extend your stroll to. It is a fabulous site to see, as its name suggests!

(10) Enjoy a lazy day in the sun at one of Chicago's beaches

Lake Michigan and its shores in the Chicago Metropolis provide a lot of relaxing beaches throughout the area. There are beaches off of Lakeshore Drive downtown, Beaches in Lincoln Park, Evanston and so many other suburbs of Chicago. If you choose a beach downtown there are a lot of boating and sightseeing activities you can sign up for and take part in right there! You can also have lunch or dinner on a boat cruise right off the beach on Lake Michigan. A good example of an available lunch or dinner cruise is on ' The Spirit of Chicago'.

(11) Visit and Tour a world renowned University Campus:-
   A few examples are:-
   - The University of Chicago
   - Northwestern University.

– Columbia College

The University of Chicago has a campus downtown and gives tours. You can easily take a stroll around their beautiful downtown campus on your own or you can schedule a tour. Either way, you will be impressed by their beautiful campus.

Northwestern University has its undergraduate campus in Evanston. This is a stone throw from downtown Chicago. In fact, you can see the Chicago skyline in the distance from its gorgeous campus! Lake Michigan borders the entire Evanston Campus and there are beautiful beaches everywhere! Northwestern has an extremely impressive campus with Division 1 level athletic facilities, brand new dormitories, a World Class Theater and outstanding colleges all in a loving neighborhood that feels like home.

Columbia College Chicago is situated in two or three of the skyscrapers right in the heart of the city. The dormitories are right there with access to every facet of the city life any student chooses to partake of. It is a fantastic College mostly focused on media arts and business. Its beauty is the beauty of the city it is surrounded by.

There are a handful of other colleges and universities in the metropolis!

(12) United Center

The United Center is home to the Chicago Bulls. One can schedule to go and see a game, watch a concert or simply tour the famous building situated downtown Chicago.

All year round there are A-list musicians performing at the United Center. Catch one of your favorites one of the evenings you are visiting Chicago. Also, if you are in Chicago during basketball season, it would be exciting to buy a ticket and catch a Bulls game on their home turf.

(13) The Shedd Aquarium- The Shedd Aquarium is a world renowned aquarium. It is known for its sea life, penguin performances and 4D shows. By 4D shows, I mean that if it is snowing in the movie, it will be snowing on you in the theater! If someone is startled in the movie, you may jump back startled in your seat in the theater! This is how vivid the Shedd Aquarium movies experiences are! It is thrilling!

(14) Navy Pier and Museum Day - Visit the Navy Pier downtown Chicago and pick a museum or two to visit. Navy Pier has a lot of food and family friendly activities. Navy Pier is the best spot to book a boat ride or a cruise from downtown Chicago.

There are a good number of notable museums downtown for you to choose from. Here are a few of them;-
    -Chicago's Children's Museum
    - Museum of Science and Industry
    - Art Institute of Chicago
    -Field Museum,
    - Adler Planetarium

(15) Go on a helicopter ride and view the entire city from above.

This is a wonderful idea that needs to be booked at least two days before you plan on taking the tour. It is a surreal view of the city! People look like ants on the ground and cars look like match boxes! It is hilarious!

It is not a day long trip but you are going to feel like relaxing in your hotel room on solid ground after you do this! CHE Tours is one of the great companies that gives helicopter tours. The Chicago Helicopter Experience.

(16) Visit The Guaranteed Rate Field

This field was formerly known as US Cellular Field and even earlier, Comiskey Park. This Field is home to the White Sox baseball team. If it is baseball season, purchase a ticket and watch a game! There are many perks to going to the field to watch a game. If you are a fan that likes to play baseball or you have a little leaguer in your family, you can use the batting cages and other game practicing equipment put up for the fans by the Whitesox to enjoy during the breaks and halftime. All of those perks are almost as exciting as watching the game! If it is not game season just visit the field to experience its awesomeness!

(17) Soldiers Field

Home of the Chicago Cubs! Buy tickets and watch a Cubs game!

During the off season, Soldiers field can be rented out for different types of parties and celebrations. Before Soldiers Field, the Cubs used Wrigley's Field as their home.

(18) Go to a Festival

Depending on the time of the year, there is usually a festival going on somewhere in the Metropolis! Here are some examples of great festivals to attend:-

Lollapalooza Chicago

Taste of Chicago

Chicago Jazz Festival

And lots more!

(19) Watch a movie at an AMC Dine-in theater

This is a great experience! The chairs are much larger and much more comfortable than regular movie theater seats. Waiters come in and serve you dinner and dessert as the movie progresses! It is a healthy combination of a movie theater and a classy restaurant with your favorite foods!

(20) Take a stroll down The Chicago Riverwalk.

The Chicago Riverwalk is an uninterrupted pedestrian trail along the south bank of the Chicago River in downtown Chicago. It is an easy way to soak up the beauty of the Chicago river and the restaurants and buildings around it!

There you have it! This book does not even come close to touching on all the tourist attractions in the Chicago Metropolis but it is definitely a great start! Please take as many pictures and home movies as you can. You are going to want to live this experience over and over again as you look through your pictures and watch your videos! There is no other experience quite like visiting the windy city or 'Chi Town' as it is often referred to as. Make this book your companion during your trip and you can't go wrong!

If this book has been of value to you, I would love it if you left a favorable review for the book on amazon.

CITATIONS

The Bean (Cloud Gate) in Chicago. (2012, July 6). Choose Chicago. Retrieved August 3, 2022, from https://www.choosech icago.com/articles/tours-and-attractions/the-bean-chicago/

Chicago Riverwalk. (2017, August 29). Enjoy Illinois. Retrieved August 3, 2022, from https://www.enjoyillinois.com/plan-your -trip/

About the Author

ICON is an enigma.